"In Pursuit of His Will: *The Journey of Finding True Love*"

Marquitta Rodgers

"In Pursuit of His Will: The Journey of Finding True Love"

Copyright © 2014 Marquitta Rodgers

All rights reserved. No portion of the book may be reproduced or utilized in any form or by any means, electronic or mechanical, including photocopying, recording, or by any other information storage and retrieval system, without permission in writing from the author.

Scripture taken from the New King James Version and New International Version. Copyright © 1973, 1978, 1984 by International Bible Society. Used by permission.

ISBN-13: 978-0692286715

Dedication

I would first like to dedicate this book to my daughter, Briana. Thirteen years ago you changed my life for the better and I never knew that bringing a life into this world could bless my life as much as you have. My prayer for you is that you will develop into a woman of purpose who will walk in covenant with Christ all the days of your life. You are my motivation for everything I do (aside from God) and I love you more than words can express.

To my mother, Arnater, it is because of your prayers and intercession for my life that I have become the woman I am today. You have sacrificed everything for my sisters and I, and I am so grateful that God hand-picked you to be my mom. You have had the greatest influence in my life! Thank you for being the example of how to live a lifestyle of prayer, intercession and serving God. I love you so much, Mom!

To my sisters, Frenda, Victoria and Danyil, God could not have chosen better sisters to place in my life. Thank you for your unconditional love for me and for always being my greatest supporters. I love you!

Lastly, I would like to thank my spiritual parents, Drs. Matthew and Kamilah Stevenson, for helping me to see myself the way God does and for never giving up on me. Thank you for imparting, sowing and investing in my life over the last 8 years. You both have impacted my life greatly and I am grateful God sent you into my life exactly when He did. I love you Stevensons!

Table of Contents

Dedication 3

Foreword by: *Kamilah Stevenson* 6

Introduction 9

Chapter 1: *The Undefined Relationship* 12

Chapter 2: *Convenient Relationships vs. Covenant Relationships* 21

Chapter 3: *Discerning the Counterfeit* 27

Chapter 4: *HE who Finds…* 35

Chapter 5: *There is Purpose in Waiting on God's Timing* 40

Chapter 6: *Discovering the Blessings and Benefits in the Life of an Unmarried Believer* 45

Chapter 7: *A Season of Unavailability* 52

Chapter 8: *Dating vs. Courtship* 61

Chapter 9: *Boundaries, Transparency & Accountability* 68

Chapter 10: *In Pursuit of His Will* 78

Closing: *"Prayers for the Unmarried"* 85

Foreword

In our day and age, the topic of knowing what to do as a single man or woman and how to serve your life before the Lord is a much needed topic that must be taught. The Word of God tells the seasoned woman to teach what is good and that is exactly what is uncovered with profound wisdom while journeying 'In Pursuit of His Will'.

This book is for every unmarried person who wants to learn how to live a life that is un-distracted before the Lord. There are indeed benefits to singleness and their revelation teaches the single man and woman how to triumph in this distinct season of life. This is particularly difficult for single women to do especially because of the emotional ties with marital dreams and a strong desire for family. In the reality of this inner conflict that women must overcome, Marquitta helps the single woman to know that she is in the midst of the greatest opportune time to take advantage of an undivided heart before God. In marriage, one must skillfully learn how to relate to God in the midst of family life. This is something that married women must grow into. However, as a single woman you have the availability and flexibility unlike that of one who is in a committed covenant of that magnitude. Each situation and position has its advantages and its restrictions, but the greatest thing that

Christians can do is live in the blessed realm of whatever circumstance they find themselves in. This book helps to disciple the unmarried into the practicalities of this truth.

One of those practicalities includes my favorite chapter of this book, Chapter 3, which speaks of learning to discern a counterfeit. Marquitta helps Christians to sharpen their discernment so that they do not become the target of a counterfeit. This is highly important in a time when it has become difficult for believers to distinguish the truth from a lie. Satan is determined to kill, steal, and destroy all that God has purposed us to be; because of this we must recognize when he is sending someone to carry out his plans, whether that particular individual knows that he/she is part of this plan or not. The most important part is that we know when someone is sent to play a part in destroying and interfering with our future.

This final thing I would like to highlight is the exceptional way the author interweaves throughout the book the need to have Godly perspective as an unmarried individual. Perspective is important because it dictates the way we respond to our circumstance and situation. God wants us to respond in a way that shows our thankfulness and gratitude towards wherever we find ourselves in life that is ordained by Him. We can easily do this as long as we submit ourselves to HIM and follow HIS path. This ensures us of a fruitful and productive life; it also causes us to feel comforted in knowing that, wherever we stand in life, whether we are married or single, we find confidence in God that there is no greater place for us to be at that moment. Marquitta helps to unravel this revelation, and helps to put the Body of Christ on a path that prepares women for womanhood and encourages men towards godly adjustments. She encourages all of the unmarried to be prepared for what God has created them to be and do in this life without ungodly interruption or intrusion.

Apostle Kamilah Stevenson

Introduction

If you ask the average unmarried believer what their beliefs or standards for dating are, you will most likely receive various responses. Some believe it is okay to date 'randomly', while others believe dating is okay as long as it is exclusive between two individuals. Others have adopted the idea of casually dating, which can be defined as dating in open relationships where there is no commitment. Many believers approach dating the same way as the rest of the world and do not believe there is a standard for dating. Dating has become a casual interaction that can include two or more individuals. It can be exclusive or non-exclusive. One person could have deeper feelings than the other person in the relationship or one could be more interested in moving to the 'next level' while the other person is content with where they are. There are different forms of dating and the definition varies from person to person.

As I reflected on why many relationships fail, how believers consistently fall into sexual sin, why more and more children are born out of wedlock, and why many relationships never reach the engagement or marriage stage, I realized it is partially a result of how believers approach and entertain their relationships. When it comes to the average believer, there is no distinction made between their beliefs and the beliefs of unbelievers concerning their reasons or standards for pursing relationships. However, I believe if those who are lovers of Christ will understand God has standards, principles and a purpose for their lives; they will approach relationships His way. God is concerned about every aspect of our lives including who we choose to be in relation with or marry. Unless Godly standards are acknowledged and upheld, we will continue to see the negative effects that are produced from relationships that are not submitted to, governed by or ordained by God.

Before any believer enters into a potential relationship, it is imperative that God is consulted and the question of whether or not you are ready to enter into a relationship should be proposed. The word of God tells us, *"In all your ways know, recognize, and acknowledge Him and He will direct and make straight and plain your paths"* (Proverbs 3:6). Some believers argue that there is no biblical reference for dating or courtship. Although neither word is listed in the bible, there are several scriptural references and principles that serve as a guide and a model for unmarried believers, as well as how they are to approach pursuing or entertaining relationships. In this book, we will review biblical principles and references that believers should embrace as it pertains to the issues of dating, courtship and relationships.

Chapter 1: The Undefined Relationship

Would you invest your time, energy or finances in a college program for four years knowing you would not be awarded a degree or any form of official certification at the end? Would you agree to consistently pay a car note every month for five years and at the end of paying the full cost of the car, you have to return it to the dealership? If not, why would you invest your time, energy and finances in a relationship that has no potential of going anywhere? It is imperative that you define every friendship, relationship or potential relationship before jumping into it. Defining your relationships early on will help you to determine if the relationship is worth pursuing/entertaining. If your relationships are undefined, you risk the possibility of not receiving what you need, causing excessive confusion, disappointment and miscommunication and the relationship will most likely not grow or evolve into anything more than what it started out to be.

There are several dangers of entertaining undefined relationships. One of the most common dangers is that one or both parties in the relationship will eventually get hurt when the reality sets in that the other person is not as committed, does not desire a 'monogamous' relationship or does not desire marriage in the future. It is unwise to enter into a new relationship without any expectations and without defining the purpose of the relationship. Another danger of undefined relationships is there are no real boundaries set in place. Since there are no set expectations, it is impossible to establish any real boundaries because each person is free to do whatever they want with whomever they want. When there are no established expectations, it leaves both individuals assuming that the other person understands what they want or do not want in the relationship. Confusion and miscommunication will become the theme of the relationship and it may be short lived once the couple finally expresses their intentions and desires for the relationship.

      Some other terms for undefined relationships are 'just hanging out', 'talking', 'seeing each other' or 'getting to know one another'. Getting to know someone just as a friend is great and should be the initial step before entering into a relationship. However, if boundaries are crossed and the friendship turns into going out on dates alone, having in-depth conversations about creating a possible future together, talking on the phone for countless hours (and in the midnight hours), holding hands, hugging, kissing, entertaining 'sweet talk' or having sex, boundaries are automatically crossed into the relationship level. Even if it is not acknowledged as a official relationship by both individuals, one person will most likely believe they are in a relationship. Those who are not actually looking for a committed relationship but participate in relationship-related activities will argue they are not in a relationship, but soul ties will have already begun to develop between the two (even if sex is not involved at this point).

When relationships are undefined, there is no clear agreement between the two persons involved about what is expected in the relationship or what are the needs of each person. In this case, assumption becomes the foundation of the relationship and one or both people involved at some point will become hurt, disappointed or offended due to the lack of defining what they need or expect in the relationship.

For those who secretly look for 'friends with benefits' relationships, it is typical for them to avoid defining their relationships. Have you ever witnessed a man or woman who avoids labeling their relationship or discussing anything that will officially bind them to another person? This type of person should be avoided if you intend to have a covenant relationship and for it to potentially move forward into the engagement and marriage stage. Avoidance is the most common sign that an individual is not ready for a committed relationship and they would rather use your time, energy and whatever else you could offer them without any commitment to you.

So how should you successfully define your relationships? Defining your relationship requires communication and for you to ask the right questions to get a clear understanding of what you are getting yourself into ("*Wisdom is the principal thing; therefore get wisdom: and with all thy getting get understanding*" Proverbs 4:7). Some key questions to ask depending on what kind of relationship you are defining are as follows:

"What do you expect out of this relationship/friendship?"

"What are your expectations of me or intentions with me?"

"Where would you like to see this relationship/friendship go?"

If it is discovered that both individuals have a mutual attraction and both desire to move forward into a relationship, more questions that should make or break moving forward are:

"How were your past relationships?"

"When was your last relationship?"

"Who are you accountable to?"

"Are you willing to be transparent with me?"

"What are your goals?"

"What are some things that are important to you?"

"How is your commitment level?"
"What are some of your main responsibilities?"

"How is your relationship with God?"

"What are you strengths and weaknesses?"

"Do you desire marriage in the future?"

"What kind of boundaries do you intend to set in place to protect US from moving outside of the will of God?"

"Do you want children in the future?"

Your initial meeting to find out what each person desires are not limited to the above questions. The point of having this conversation is to determine if you and the other person have basic compatibilities and if you desire and value the same things in a relationship. This step alone can save you time and energy from entering into a relationship headed nowhere.

Chapter 1: The Undefined Relationship

If you or the other person believes these questions are too invasive, it is a clear indicator you are not ready to handle a relationship. Relationships are intended to be open and transparent. Without honesty, openness and transparency, it will never grow, mature or become fruitful. Asking these questions or similar questions will reveal the heart of the person and their intentions of wanting to pursue or entertain a relationship with you. When the interest is more than friendship, these questions are important factors in determining if you or the other person has the capacity to entertain a relationship with one another. If one person in the relationship is not ready for a commitment, asking these questions will expose this issue. It will reveal the posture of their heart concerning relationships and whether or not they are ready and serious about pursuing (**only men should pursue**) or entertaining a relationship with you. After asking these series of questions (the determination stage is not limited to these few questions), it is important not to make plans to try to "fix" the other person, coach them into agreeing to be committed to you or proceed into a relationship when excessive red flags are present.

It is very common to see unmarried men and women attempting to make a woman or man their wife or husband after they have received countless numbers of red flags. This is NOT the will of God. Of course, no person will ever be perfect. However, when a person shows they are not ready to handle a commitment, you can not make them ready. Ignoring red flags do not make them go away. God allows us to see red flags to protect us and moving forward when red flags are present is like removing God's protection. Whenever red flags are present it represents a caution to STOP. What happens when we run a stop sign or red light? It causes us to violate laws as well as put other drivers and pedestrian's lives in danger!

Attempting to move forward in a relationship where it is clear that the other person is not ready for a commitment is unwise because the relationship will have a high probability of ending in disappointment. It is unhealthy to assume if you invest time, energy, finances or put 'work' into a person, they will become ready. Investing in a relationship with a man or woman who clearly shows signs of not being able to commit or is not interested in anything long term with you is like leasing or investing in a car, and at the end of the agreement, sending it back to the dealership to be purchased by someone else. It is a waste of money and time, and in the end you will have to start back at square one. This leasing mentality will not work if your intention is to someday have a lifelong commitment. Just because you invest in someone does not mean they will grow to love, value, honor or want to marry you. Asking key questions early on will determine if the person is close to or already positioned to offer you a long-term and committed covenant relationship. It will always be your choice of whether or not you want to invest in a dead end or a lifelong relationship. Choose wisely!

"In Pursuit of His Will: The Journey of Finding True Love"

Chapter 2: Convenient Relationships vs. Covenant Relationships

There is a significant difference between a man/woman who desires a *Covenant* relationship with you and one who wants a *Convenient* relationship with you. Convenient relationships are established through those who are lonely, selfish, bored, have an ungodly desire for intimacy or romance, have a strong spirit of idolatry of relationships or marriage or who are governed by lust. Convenient relationships are created when a person desires companionship, intimacy, someone to "take" from or manipulate, then looks for a person to be in an intimate relationship with (not necessarily sexual) but is not mature enough (naturally or spiritually) to entertain a committed relationship. People who look for convenient relationships usually have no intention of commitment or their perspective of commitment is dysfunctional.

Convenient relationships are based on selfishness and what a person can get out of someone else. Men and women who look for convenient relationships are typically receivers and give only when it costs them nothing. They most commonly enter into convenient relationships for sexual purposes. They only seem to show up during late night hours or when they want ungodly intimacy. Another reason people look for convenient relationships is for monetary purposes. These are usually people who need someone to live with, a car to drive, money or daily meals. They look to receive money and gifts by use of manipulation, victimization or simply by using another person. They typically prey on those with low self-esteem or those who have severe issues of loneliness. Emotional attachment is another reason some people pursue convenient relationships. Those with emotional instability look for ways of filling voids of loneliness; they lack love for themselves or feel loved through relationships they are not ready to handle. They often look for relationships with people who are authoritative, those who appear to resemble father or mother figures, who are overprotective, cunning with their words, or anyone who will show them attention even if it is unhealthy attention.

Convenient relationships can last any where from a few weeks to several years. Most people who entertain this type of relationship are unaware they are in one and do not see it as being dysfunctional. There are several different reasons why people enter into or pursue relationships that are convenient, but all of them are unhealthy. Those who are being used in their relationship rarely see they are being used whether it is for sex, money, emotional stability or for other reasons. If you are the only person who gives in your relationships (whether it is time, finances, emotional support...) you are likely entertaining a convenient relationship and are being used. The relationship is based on selfishness and the convenience of another.

Covenant relationships, on the other hand, are the idea of God. They are based on commitment, loyalty, faithfulness, and unconditional love. Covenant relationships are not just limited to male-female relationships and are necessary to have where ever there is a God-ordained relationship; friendship, mentorship, discipleship or marriage. If we consider the story of David and Jonathan in *1 Samuel 18:3-4,* we see the nature of their relationship was a covenant one.

"3 And Jonathan made a covenant with David because he loved him as himself. 4 Jonathan took off the robe he was wearing and gave it to David, along with his tunic, and even his sword, his bow and his belt."

The foundation for covenant relationships is selflessness. In covenant relationships, the desire to give to the other person far exceeds the desire to receive from them. Although we no longer have to go through the same ritual ceremony Jonathan and David did, the principles and concepts of covenant remains the same. Selflessness, Honor, Respect, Commitment, Faithfulness, Honesty, Loyalty, Oneness, Sensitivity, Accountability, Transparency and

Unconditional Love are all attributes found in Covenant Relationships. We see that both friends were more than willing to sacrifice for each other.

As it pertains to relationships that exceed beyond friendship or that have the agenda of marriage, those who understand covenant understand it is not their relationship that fulfills them. Their fulfillment comes from God. They establish a covenant with the one who is "True Love", Jesus Christ, and he in return teaches them how to be faithful and committed to him in order to become prepared to do the same for their future mate. Covenant must first be learned through our relationship with Christ then it can be modeled later within our relationships.

The main prerequisite for marriage is having a covenant heart and mindset. If marriage is your desire, you must follow covenant principles in your potential or current relationship. You can not enter into a convenient relationship with a man or woman who is not the will of God for your life and expect a God ordained marriage to come from it. Convenient relationships will never have the potential to grow or evolve in to anything lasting because it is not the intent or nature of the relationship to do so. If it ever develops into a marriage, the fruit of the marriage will be hindered drastically because it will be based on the foundation of selfishness and convenience. Although a convenient relationship can last for quite some time, it will eventually become a endless cycle of one person in the relationship attempting to make the other person walk in covenant with them when it is clearly not their desire or within their ability to do so. Waiting on God and his timing, along with allowing God to instill covenant principles within you, will ensure you will not waste time in dead-end and convenient relationships. Despite what society tells you, it is possible to have a covenant relationship which is based on love, faithfulness and commitment. You do not have to settle for anything less!

"In Pursuit of His Will: The Journey of Finding True Love"

Chapter 3: Discerning the Counterfeit

A counterfeit is defined as a person who is an imposture, imitation, deceitful or not real. It is one who pretends to be someone or something they are not. Some counterfeits intentionally attempt to deceive others. They act as or portray themselves to be a *"type"* of person with specific characteristics and qualities that they truthfully do not embody. We often see counterfeits that attend church and can quote the word of God backwards and forward but lack a true understanding or reverence for the word of God. Many of these men and women have been raised in church and understand *"church lingo"*, however; their lives have yet to be transformed and governed by Christ. Their motives and intentions are selfish, impure and ungodly. Counterfeits look for those who are weak, uncertain, unstable, feeble, anxious, desperate, insecure and lack identity. They can identify individuals with these characteristics because the same weaknesses are present in them. Their goal is to enter into relationships with men/women for their own personal gain and to fulfill their selfish needs.

Counterfeits do not always come in the form of an evil person, wolf in sheep's clothing, or a person who purposely deceives others. Counterfeits are sometimes deceived about their reality and many times do not understand or are unaware that they are in fact a counterfeit. Those who are deceived often attempt to enter into relationships prematurely for the sake of not wanting to be alone. They often take baggage and soul ties from previous relationships into their new ones. Most counterfeits who enter into new relationships have never taken the time to self-reflect, evaluate and receive healing from prior hurts and failed relationships. They are not mature enough to have a covenant relationship and have not learned to love or value himself/herself.

Even if the person does not premeditate being deceitful or hurtful to someone else, they have by default, become a counterfeit because they are attempting to enter into a relationship prematurely without the ability to walk in covenant with someone else. This does not make them a bad person, but they can be identified as a counterfeit because they will be a detriment to themselves, anyone who they attempt to date and their relationships, until they gain the self-awareness and truth of where they really are in that area of their life. They must submit to a season of healing, learning who they are and must allow God to prepare them to become ready to entertain a potential relationship.

How can you identify a counterfeit? You can identify a counterfeit similarly to how you

Chapter 3: Discerning the Counterfeit

would identify a counterfeit 100 dollar bill. You examine it and pay close attention to the details of the bill. When you just look at the outer surface of the bill quickly, it can be easily mistaken as a real 100 dollar bill. Examining a counterfeit person is quite similar. If he or she is *"churched"*, they will know the surface things to say and behaviors. They are charming with their words and often can tell you what you want to hear. Counterfeits will almost always attract men/women, who are insecure, anxious, have low self-esteem, are unstable or who lack identity. They rarely attempt to approach those who are confident, stable and secure.

When examining counterfeits, you must look beyond their surface. Their substance (or lack thereof) is what matters most. When determining if a 100 dollar bill is a counterfeit after the surface of the bill is inspected, it is held up to the light. When we apply this method to people, we must examine them and their lives in the light (naturally and spiritually). This method should automatically rule out men/women who only come around at night time. They can not be accurately measured in the dark and most often, they will be appear to be the real thing because you will lack sufficient light to be able to accurately see. When attempting to determine the true state of a person, it is important to have FOCUS! It is difficult to focus in the dark. When viewing the bill in the light, you can accurately see the colors and watermark embedded in it. The same can be said when you examine men/women in the light. In most cases, you will be able to see their true nature and the fruit or the absence of fruit in their lives.

Sometimes when examining bills in the light, counterfeits slip through the natural light check. The next and final step is to examine it under an ultraviolet light. Ultraviolet light can detect and reveal what is invisible to the human eye. It exposes what is beneath the surface and the true state of a thing. Discernment and the Holy Spirit can be compared to an ultraviolet light. Both resources help us to see beneath the surface and the inward state of people. Discernment is necessary because it reveals the truth in what our flesh, intelligence and natural eye can not see. Discernment is a spiritual wisdom that comes from God and it is gained through our relationship and interactions with Christ *(***1 Corinthians 1:18-31***)*. The word of God tells us discernment and wisdom is developed through training and righteousness *(Philippians 1:9, Hebrews 5:11-14)*. Without discernment, you will become a target for counterfeits.

The Holy Spirit reveals all things in due time. **1 Corinthians 2:10** teaches us:

"Yet to us God has unveiled and revealed them by and through His Spirit, for the

[Holy] Spirit searches diligently, exploring and examining everything, even sounding the profound and bottomless things of God [the divine counsels and things hidden and beyond man's scrutiny]."

The word of God also tells us in **John 16:13:**

"But when he, the Spirit of truth, comes, he will guide you into all the truth. He will not speak on his own; he will speak only what he hears, and he will tell you what is yet to come."

The Holy Spirit is the revealer of all truth. So if the Holy Spirit reveals the truth in us as well as others, how can you determine a counterfeit without the Holy Spirit? Those who lack the help of the Holy Spirit will find it difficult to determine if a person is sent in their lives from heaven or hell and will likely find themselves in reoccurring cycles of falling for counterfeits. Having the Holy Spirit on the inside of you will activate your ability to discern a counterfeit who has attempted to enter into your life.

Counterfeits come in different shapes, forms, backgrounds and genders. They do not all speak or behave the same but there are some common behaviors to be aware of. Some signs (not limited to these) to determine if you are in a relationship with a COUNTERFEIT are:

~ He/She draws you away from God.

~ He/She enjoys ungodly activities (i.e. fornication, oral sex...).

~ He/She has no true accountability in their life.

~ He/She is evasive about their past.

~ He/She is often attached to several people of the opposite sex and labels them as their "friends" even when there is an obvious attraction to those deemed as friends.

~ He/She has proven to be dishonest.

~ He/She always makes excuses about wanting to keep your relationship private (meaning they don't want others to know it exists).

~ He/She is extremely secretive.

~ He/She is uninterested in conversations about commitment.

~ He/She would rather be alone than in group/family settings or is disinterested in getting to know your family and friends.

~ He/She is insensitive towards you and your feelings.

~ He/She often shows signs of selfishness.

~He/She has proven to be dishonest.

~He/She always makes excuses to break promises.

Unmarried men and women, not only is it important that you have discernment and the Holy Spirit to identify counterfeits when they attempt to enter into your life, but it is equally important to make sure YOU are not a counterfeit! Just as you examine others, their motives, character and qualities; you must honestly evaluate yourself as well to ensure you do not become the counterfeit in someone else's life. If you are not ready for the responsibility and commitment of a relationship but attempt to enter into one prematurely, you are by default considered a counterfeit. It is important that you allow God to prepare you and make you ready to become the real deal.

"In Pursuit of His Will: The Journey of Finding True Love"

Chapter 4: *HE* who *Finds...*

"He who finds a wife finds a good thing and obtains favor from the LORD."

(Proverbs 18:22 ESV)

If the word of God tells us "He who finds a wife finds a good thing and obtains favor from the LORD", why does a large population of Christian women believe it is their responsibility to go out and find and pursue a man? Society's belief is that if a woman is not dating or in a relationship, something is wrong with her. Women who are dating are most certainly in the spotlight and the talk of headlines. The same can be said in today's churches. Dating seems like the popular thing to do and women have become desperate to go out and find them someone to date or to make their husband because they are believed to be insignificant without a man. We often see Christian women entering into unhealthy relationships, relationships with men who they are unequally yoked with, or in relationships before they are well prepared themselves. They have lost the need to be prepared to enter covenant relationships and to wait on God to send them a man who is compatible and suitable for them to enter into a relationship with. It is common to see Christian women dating men who do not belong to a local church, are not passionate about God and in many cases do not have a personal relationship with Jesus at all. So many women have become discouraged. They don't believe the right man will ever find them and feel they will be unmarried for the rest of their lives. In efforts to make sure that this does not become their reality, they take drastic measures of settling for men who they were never intended to enter into relationships with or go out seeking to find anyone who seem available.

The common questions that many unmarried Christian women are often plagued with is, "Where is my Boaz?" and, "When will I find him?" They are looking for the church, prophetic words, friends, family, media, society or whoever has the answer to this question. The answer is simple: **WHEN YOU STOP LOOKING FOR HIM!** If women do not use the word of God as a standard for their lives, their relationships will resemble those of the world. The word of God is perfectly clear, He who finds a wife, not she who finds a husband! This means as women, we are not to go out searching for men (saved or unsaved) to date or marry.

Many of us have witnessed women *"church hop"* in order to find a man when there are none available in their local church, but this method usually ends up in disaster. It is the man's job to search for and choose his wife. As the intended head of the relationship/marriage/

Chapter 4: HE who Finds...

family, it is important that he takes the leading role in choosing his wife by first making sure he is spiritually, naturally, emotionally, physically and financially prepared and has spiritual discernment to discover the woman who is capable of being his helpmate. If the woman looks for or pursues him, the foundation of the relationship will be built on her leading the relationship, which was never intended by God.

There was purpose in God creating Adam before Eve. Adam's role was to lead her; however, when we review **Genesis chapter 3**, Eve took on the leadership role in the relationship, which she was never created to do. Instead of submitting to the voice of God and her husband, her actions were influenced by the serpent/Satan. This caused their roles to be reversed and instead of Adam leading his wife to follow God's instructions, Eve led her husband into disobedience and dishonor to God. Not only did both Adam and Eve suffer from not standing in their rightful roles, their seed suffered later. Just like there was purpose in why Adam was to lead Eve, there is purpose in why God instructed men to search out and find their wives...not the other way around.

So, if men are responsible for going out to find/search for their wives, what is the role of the woman? I'm glad you asked! Although a greater emphasis is placed on the role of men finding their wife, the role of women is equally important. The role of the Christian unmarried woman is to wait on the Lord. In the next chapter, we will review what it really means to *"wait on the Lord".*

Chapter 4: HE who Finds…

Chapter 5: There is Purpose in Waiting on God's Timing

We live in a society where we do not enjoy waiting and often gravitate towards the things we want and can get *"right now"*. However, it is a proven fact that waiting can produce quality results. If you don't believe me, try putting an unseasoned steak in the microwave. It may cook quickly on the outer surface, but the center will be uncooked and it will be tasteless. Furthermore, microwaving a steak will ruin the quality of it. On the other hand, giving it the right seasonings and cooking it on the stove or in the oven will take a longer time to cook, but the steak will be at its best quality when prepared correctly. The same principle can be applied to relationships. Waiting may not seem enjoyable but when a man/woman is prepared while waiting for the right relationship, it will produce quality results when the right relationship presents itself.

We often hear people say *"Singles need to wait on the Lord"*, but what does it mean to wait on the Lord as it pertains to relationships, dating, courtship and marriage? One definition of "wait" is *"to stay in a place or remain in readiness or in anticipation (until something expected happens or for someone to arrive or catch up); to be ready or at hand"*. Sometimes when the word wait is heard, it is believed to mean staying in a position while doing nothing until a certain time or until something occurs. However, when we use and hear the phrase *"to wait on the Lord"*, it often requires specific actions or behaviors while we wait. A key term used in the mentioned definition of wait is *readiness*. The word readiness is derived from ready; which means to be *prepared*. Unmarried believers who desire to be married are taught to just wait on God until he sends their mate, attend church, stay saved and trust God to send their mate when He is ready. The problem with this belief is that 9 out of 10 times, God is waiting for unmarried believers to become ready to send their mate. He longs to see healthy marriages that will glorify him! Many men and women are waiting for the day when they will find their earthly love or be found but often miss the preparation stage which precedes being found or finding the right one. Waiting on the Lord to send a mate requires preparation.

The preparation stage is always required prior to entering into a relationship with someone. Although, the preparation stage is a critical one, unmarried men and women often ignore it or when they do attempt to begin a season of preparation, it ends prematurely. In *Proverbs 24:27,* the word of God instructs us to prepare first, and then build a house. A person or couple can not attempt to build a house or a relationship before they are prepared. When relationships are built backwards they do not last long or experience several unnecessary obstacles due to having a weak foundation.

Preparation before relationships and marriage require both men and women to be delivered from strongholds that have the power to be detrimental to the individual, their purpose and others. It requires, pruning, unlearning ungodly beliefs and generational dysfunctions, submission to God and his will for your life, healing from past relationships, hurts, disappointments and receiving a level of restoration to become sober with a new mindset and Godly perspectives. In the preparation stage, girls are transformed into women and boys are made into men. Women learn how to become wives and men learn how to become husbands. The preparation stage will not make you perfect, but it will make you ready for a healthy and lasting relationship.

If you have taken the necessary time for God to mature, heal and prepare you to become a husband or wife, refuse to settle as a result of being tired of waiting on the right one. Settling is proof that your trust is not in God to do what he has already promised you. When your trust, faith and hope is truly in the Lord, there is no need or desire to settle! When your trust is in Christ Jesus, you begin to see waiting as a benefit instead of a curse, God's timing as protection instead of a punishment and most importantly, you begin to understand you can not afford to settle for anyone who has the potential to compromise your purpose or future. Until you understand the blessings in your *"waiting season"*, you will never enjoy the quality of your life and purpose in being an unmarried believer! There is purpose in why you are still unmarried and until you discover it, chances are you will remain unmarried or settle for someone who was never intended to be a part of your life. Your happiness or unhappiness as an unmarried believer is your choice. The choice is always yours to move prematurely into a relationship/marriage or to wait and submit to God's timing for your future relationship and marriage. In a world where waiting is shunned and mocked as a believer, you must remain planted in the word of God and trust his will and plans for your life!

"Wait for the Lord; Be strong, and let your heart take courage; Yes, wait for the Lord."

Psalms 27: 14

"In Pursuit of His Will: The Journey of Finding True Love"

Chapter 6: Discovering the Blessings and Benefits in the Life of an Unmarried Believer

A few years ago, I was challenged and frustrated because it had been over 3 years since I was in a relationship. Negative thoughts such as, *"There are no Godly men around who are compatible with me", "I only attract guys who are unequally yoked", " God, why would you place a love and passion in me for kids and family values if I'm never going to have a family", " I feel like I'm being hidden"* and, *"Lord, why place a desire in me to be married, when it seems as if I will never get married?"*. I became frustrated and told myself I was going back to my old self of being closed off to the idea of marriage and relationships to protect myself from disappointment. I confessed that I would block out the idea of getting married and having a family because it seemed so far fetched at the time. I went to bed that night feeling very discouraged even though I had much to be grateful for. I built a façade and acted like I did not care about getting married and having a family, when in my heart I wanted it so much.

One evening when God had my attention, he spoke to me by saying, *"Is there anything too hard for me?"* I responded by saying, *"No, but why is it taking you so long"*. This time God responded by saying, *"What is taking you so long? I am waiting on you"*. I sat in silence and pondered on his response. As I opened myself up to see what God wanted to show me, he revealed that he wanted me to go deeper in my relationship with him and required more from my life. *"What does all this mean?"* I asked him. He revealed to me that I had been hidden in a place of obscurity for my protection and he expressed his deep love for me and my future. God began to reveal my purpose for being unmarried. He had me read a passage from Jack Frost's book *"Experiencing Father's Embrace".* He told me to turn to page 41 and this is what I read:

"You were created in God's image, and God is love. If you are uncomfortable with God, you are uncomfortable with love. If you are uncomfortable with love, you are uncomfortable with yourself. If you are uncomfortable with yourself, you are going to be uncomfortable with others. If you do not believe you are lovable, you may find it difficult to receive God's gift of unmerited love and favor. And it may be difficult to enjoy healthy relationships with others if you view yourself differently from the way God views you."

Reading this was difficult to digest. God continued to minister to me about how he wanted to show me another level of his love, how to receive his love and how to love from a heart motivated and provoked by his. He had me revisit the past 15 years of my life and showed me that I developed an unconscious concept of conditional love. Although, I thought I had improved in many areas of showing love, God wanted me to unlearn my way of loving through works, doing for others but receiving nothing and through conditions. He desired to teach me how to love through his unconditional love. He also shared with me his need for me to increase in my level of intimacy with him. I measured how my intimacy level had increased from previous times but God was requiring much more! He desired for me to spend more time in his presence to learn more about who he is, his likes and dislikes and his nature. Without the process of me learning how to love and receive his unconditional love, it would be impossible for me to receive and to love his son (my future husband) the way he desires for me to. He also took me back to this same process he had began in me years ago but I moved out of it prematurely, which resulted in me revisiting the same cycles.

     I encourage all of my unmarried sisters and brothers to submit to a season of finding out what God is requiring of you. We often become frustrated with him and ask what is he waiting on and why is he taking so long when he is waiting on you to completely submit every area of your life to him that is not submitted or that is partially submitted. You can not allow your desires to drown out what he desires for your life. Many of the things you desire are a part of his plan for your life however, you cannot take the short cut to get there. I am sure many of you can see the result of moving prematurely and out of God's timing in your past relationships or in the unhealthy relationships around you.

Through my encounter with God, I was enlightened of the blessings and benefits in being unmarried and moving in God's timing. Unmarried believers often view being unmarried as a curse or punishment; however, there are several blessings in being unmarried. Even if you will be married in a later season it is important to embrace where you are now and understand the significance of why you are unmarried. Some blessings and opportunities that unmarried believers have the privilege of taking advantage of are, but not limited to:

1) Enjoying more free time to complete your endeavors before marriage…school, career, traveling etc.

2) More time to focus on building our relationship with God. **(1 Corinthians 7:32-34)**

3) More time to learn who we are and our identity in Christ.

4) More time to develop skills for covenant relationships.

5) Becoming disciplined and balanced in our daily living.

6) Utilizing the necessary time to become a wife or a husband. A wife or husband is not created once you say I do but is established before marriage.

When we are so focused on the who, when, how and why, we often miss the blessing of allowing God to figure out the details while we walk in what he has purposed us to. I truly believe God desires to raise up those who are willing to focus on their growth and development, becoming disciplined, matured, selfless, being delivered, restored and walking in a new level of wholeness before marriage. Those who will allow his timing to be the standard; not your biological clocks, not comparing yourself to others around you or the need to check the accomplishment of marriage off of your list. For many of you, he desires to teach you balance so that when the time comes for marriage, you do not neglect him or your assignment.

I have learned the best thing I can do for my future husband is submit to and invest in my relationship with Jesus in order to allow him to transform me into the mother, wife, counselor, deliverer and intercessor he has created me to be. Submitting to your season of growth, development, maturity and preparation is imperative so that, ladies, when you are ready to be found, your future husband will find his good thing. Gentlemen, on the other hand, submitting to your season of being unmarried is necessary to become the man and husband God desires for you to be. This season is critical for you so when God gives you the green light to find your wife, you already have the Godly qualities of a husband. Until then, it is beneficial for unmarried men and women to receive and embrace the blessings and opportunities of being unmarried while God is behind the scenes writing your love story.

Chapter 6: Discovering the Blessings and Benefits in the Life of an Unmarried Believer

Chapter 7: A Season of Unavailability

Desiring relationships and marriage more than desiring God can open doors for counterfeits to enter your life. Just as God knows your heart's desires, so does the enemy. He sends men/women who know just enough of the Word of God and knows how to *"play church"* in order to get their foot in the door. If your desire for marriage has become an idol in your heart, your discernment will be weakened and any man or woman who comes into your life and says they are sent by God will be a temptation for you. Soon after, you will find yourself falling deep into their trap.

When you crave the attention of men/women, it is a clear indicator you are not ready for a relationship or marriage. Anything that we crave more than God becomes an idol in our heart and thoughts. The Word of God instructs us to flee from any form of idolatry (**1 Corinthians 10:14**). If it is difficult to focus on God now and desire him above everything else, how much more would you abandon him if you had a man/woman in your life? Our desire for God must exceed our desire for a husband/wife. Unfaithfulness to God will most likely lead to unfaithfulness to an earthly man/woman. How you respond to God's love for you is a clear indicator of how you will respond to a man's/woman's love for you. If you take God's love for granted and do not value it, it will be difficult to receive or value the love from others.

When you become aware that idolatry of relationships or marriage is resident in you, it is important to remove yourself from the market of dating/courtship. It is imperative that you do so in order to give God his rightful place in your heart and life as your first priority. God can not be the priority in your life if other idols are present and vying for your heart, mind, affections and attention. It is either one or the other. One important sign that a man/woman is ready for an earthly love is the position they place God in their life. If it is difficult to put God first now while you are unmarried, he will be pushed off of your list of priorities when a man/woman is present in your life. It is God's desire that every unmarried person who desires marriage learn to make him the first priority in their life so that he can become the center and focus of their lives. Without taking the necessary time to put God in his rightful place in your life, your decisions, attitudes and behaviors will most likely be influenced by your flesh. Take the time you need off the dating/courtship market to allow God to cleanse your heart from idols and any other issue that can destroy your future relationships.

Desiring marriage is great and is the design of God. However, if marriage is a desire of your heart you must first become prepared to handle the weight of a marriage before making yourself available for a relationship. When you feel that you are ready to handle a relationship, it is important that you assess your posture and where you really are in your life. In addition to your own personal assessment, you should have some authority figure in your life to help measure your level of readiness for a relationship and marriage. We tend to have a biased assessment of ourselves so you will need the perspective of someone who knows you well and who will not be biased in their assessment of you. Having someone else in your life who can accurately assess your level of readiness and a potential relationship that you may want to entertain, can help to save you time, energy, disappointment and heartache. Having an accurate assessment of yourself, will help you to identify if you are ready for a relationship or if you need more time in your season of unavailability.

"Are You Really Ready for a New Relationship or Marriage???"

Although, no one will ever be perfect, when entering into a new relationship or marriage there are some indicators that are evident when a man or woman is not ready to enter into a relationship or marriage. Some indicators (but not limited to) are as follows:

1. **If you are SELFISH** you may not be ready for a relationship or marriage. **Relationships are give and take…not take and take. In order to grow with another individual you will have to learn how to sacrifice and give to the other person.** Whether it is your time, energy, commitment, etc. selflessness is a great characteristic of an individual who will make a good husband or wife. Selfishness is one of the number one reasons why relationships do not work out. **Selfish people do NOT make good mates.**

2. **If you have baggage from past relationships**- If you still have ill feelings towards your ex and is still affected by what they did or didn't do for you, it is a red flag to stop and not proceed into a new relationship. **When a man or woman has hurt, pain, bitterness, unforgiveness, regret and other unhealed issues from past relationships, it is inevitable they will carry these issues into their new relationship.** When hurt is present, inner vows are produced as a defense mechanism and the wounded individual does everything he/she can to prevent themselves from being hurt again. The problem with this is that a barrier and a wall is built and the heart of that individual becomes hardened to prevent anyone else from having access to it. Healing is necessary before moving forward into new relationships. **If not, you risk hurting the**

man/or woman God intended for you to love.

3. **If your have idolatry of relationships and marriage**- If a person idolizes relationships or marriage their perceptions, discernment and decision making processes is likely to be hindered and distorted. **When a man/woman desires a relationship or marriage more than they desire the will of God for their life, they will settle for anyone**. Idolatry of relationships is dangerous and it causes individuals to make poor decisions that are often detrimental to their life. It leads to ungodly cycles and soul ties from entering into relationships with the wrong people and an inability to focus on the plans of God. **Desiring relationships and marriage is a good thing, however idolizing it is not the intention of God and its offensive to him because he should be the only idol in our lives.**

While you are unmarried and in a season of "singleness" it is important to allow God to deal with any issues that has the power to negatively influence your future relationship. Learning how to become selfless, receiving healing from past relationships, allowing God to remove all ungodly idols from your heart and surrendering every area of your life to God in order to allow him to transform you into the future wife or husband he desires for you to become, is one of the best gifts you can give to your future spouse.

"It's OK to say No Thank You!"

Ladies, just because a handsome God-fearing man is present in your life does not indicate you are ready for a relationship or marriage. Gentlemen, if you have your sights on a beautiful, **Proverbs 31** woman, the best thing you could do for her is to make sure you are ready to enter into a covenant relationship with her. Entering into a relationship prematurely will eventually cause serious problems in the relationship. Both persons must be ready to handle the weight of a relationship and must exemplify some level of healing from their past relationships, family dysfunctions and ungodly perspectives and principles. Neither person will be perfect, but both individuals must be mature enough (spiritually and naturally) to entertain a relationship. A person entering into a new relationship who is immature, carrying baggage from previous relationships, has no accountability in their life, has severe heart issues, is extremely selfish or whose intent is to satisfy their own personal needs, possess qualities that indicate they are not ready for a covenant relationship.

In your season of unavailability, it is perfectly OK to exercise your *"choice"* to not be in a relationship. You do not have to take every man or woman up on their offer to *"date"* or to get to know you. If you are clearly aware that you and a potential *"boyfriend"* or *"girlfriend"* is not compatible or is not equally yoked, it is OK to say *"No Thank You"* to entertaining a relationship with them. Or, if you know you have existing soul ties from a previous relationship or heart issues, it's OKAY to voice your need to be healed before entering a new relationship. In addition, if you have had past relationships and have never intentionally taken time to self-reflect, examine, evaluate and receive healing from past hurts, disappointments and dysfunctions, it is an indicator you are not ready to move forward into a new relationship. After any break up, healing is necessary.

In order to end the cycle of entertaining unhealthy relationships, falling in love with counterfeit men/women and heart break, when presented with the opportunity to jump into a new one, learn to say *"No Thank You"*. Contrary to popular beliefs, having someone interested in you is not necessarily a sign you are ready for a new relationship. It could simply be an invitation from hell to keep you from receiving the healing you need in order to have a healthy relationship in the future. Remember Satan does not want you to walk in any level of wholeness, and will send counterfeits to play with your heart to keep you distracted from moving forward and making progress towards becoming the man/woman God has created you to be. Most of the time he will come with the same old tricks of sending a man/woman with the right height, physique and the right words to drive you down the wrong path and deeper into endless, unproductive cycles. As an unmarried individual, you have the opportunity to do something many never exercised their right to do and that is to get healed, delivered and restored while waiting on the timing of God. You can choose the path the Lord desires for you or your own! Just know there are always consequences to whatever choice you make.

"In Pursuit of His Will: The Journey of Finding True Love"

Chapter 8: Dating vs. Courtship

Dating and courtship is often confused as being the same. However, they are two different concepts and methods of entering into a relationship. Dating is when two individuals of the opposite sex seek a romantic relationship with one another. In dating relationships, the relationship is not always exclusive to two individuals. In many cases, the relationship is open for one or both parties to *"play the field"*. This type of relationship can also include the *"friends with benefits"* agreement. There is no real commitment but there may be intimacy in the relationship. However, all dating relationships are not intimate. A dating relationship can be initiated by a man or woman and last anywhere from a few days to several years. There are no set guidelines or expectations for how long the dating nature of the relationship should last or no clear intentions on moving forward to a commitment in marriage. The theme of dating is "let's go with the flow" of things and is often lead by emotions, feelings and the flesh. Dating relationships are rarely under the guidance or oversight of someone in authority and often lack accountability.

Courtship is quite the opposite of dating. It is more of an intentional agreement between two individuals to exclusively enter into a relationship. Courtship is initiated when a man pursues a woman who he is interested in getting to know on a friendship level first. Then the two enter into a covenant courtship and lastly, he asks for her hand in marriage and marries her. The man seeks approval of her father or spiritual father and submits the courtship under the authority of her father or spiritual father. Courtship takes on the position of no physical contact until marriage. The couple is rarely alone together and often spends time together in group settings to avoid crossing boundaries (we will discuss boundaries in the next chapter) and to keep their relationship honoring God.

      Courtship is goal-oriented and based on intentionality while dating typically is not. The focus and ultimate goal of courtship is to find out if the couple is compatible or suitable for marriage and the compatibility and suitability of the two is usually determined after the couple goes through the process of getting to know one another. This period of getting to know one another as friends does not include any form of activity or the crossing of boundaries, in order for both individuals to remain sober while building the authentic and genuine friendship. Courtships do not generally last long periods of time because the couple enters the relationship with the intention of either moving forward together in the engagement period or discontinuing the relationship if they are found

Chapter 8: Dating vs. Courtship

to not be compatible with or suitable for each other.

Why should you choose courtship over dating or, does it make a difference if you choose dating instead of courting? Those who date have a greater chance of ending the relationship with one or both individuals getting hurt. It can be a waste of time and there is no guarantee it will lead to finding true love. Dating has a higher probability of creating strong soul-ties that are difficult to break after the relationship ends. Dating relationships can be based solely on physical interactions and can cause one person to *"fall in love"* while the other person only desires physical contact. The danger of dating is if both people involved feel like they have "*fallen in love*" (especially when they have crossed boundaries), it will be easy for them to "*fall out of love*". When tests and trials come, it will take precedence in the relationship and the physical foundation that it has been built upon will cave in.

Some dating relationships can last for years and one or both individuals can become content with the dating relationship and never desire to move forward to make an official commitment with one another. Another common issue of dating is we often see situations where men and women are forced into marriage due to an ultimatum sometimes because a child was produced as a byproduct of the dating relationship or because it just seems like the right thing to do after the couple has played house for some time. Neither person in the relationship takes the time to consider if the person who their soul is tied with is even God's will for their life. Their choice to marry the person is solely based on fleshly reasons.

Some evident outcomes of dating are, but not limited to:

1. Selfishness
2. Soul-ties
3. UnGodly thoughts
4. Fear
5. Mistrust
6. Insecurity
7. Jealousy
8. Heart Break
9. Pride
10. Isolation from family and friends
11. Bitterness
12. Cheating
13. Indecisiveness
14. Depression
15. Reoccurring Cycles

Courtship protects both individuals from crossing boundaries and developing soul-ties. Instead, it allows the couple to truly get to know one another without the pressure of physical intimacy controlling their relationship. There is only one motive in courtship and it is for a man to find his wife. He chooses a woman who he discerns to have the qualities of his wife and courts her to confirm that she is his wife. Dating can have several motives, and although one person may have marriage in mind, the other may not.

Many people say the bible does not give reference to supporting dating or courtship; however, **1 Corinthians 7:2** says:

"Nevertheless, to avoid fornication, let every man have his own wife, and let every woman have her own husband."

This scripture supports the principle of courtship. It helps couples to avoid fornication and helps men to find their wife (**Prov. 18:22**). When we review **Matthew 7:24-27,** God speaks of a parable that compares the Christian Life with two possible ways of building a house. One house was built on sand, "Man's Way" by a foolish man who did not have the future in mind. The other house was built on solid rock, "God's Way" by a wise man who had the future in mind. The same parable can be used to compare Dating vs. Courtship. If we want a Godly relationship/marriage, we must conduct our relationships His way. As believers we can not conform to the world's ways and systems of living our lives (**Romans 12:1-2**). This also includes not allowing the world to influence our relationships and marriages!

Dating relationships are not future-focused and are rarely based on the foundation and principles of Christ. Courtship on the other hand is future-focused and Christ-centered. It is built on the nature and characteristics of Christ, commitment, faithfulness, honor, purity and marriage. The bible gives us clear instructions on how we are to live and carry ourselves as believers. Dating negates the nature and characteristics of God while Courtship supports who God is and his plan for marriage, family, relationships and Kingdom living.

Chapter 8: Dating vs. Courtship

Chapter 9: Boundaries, Transparency & Accountability

Years ago, one year after I completely gave my life to God, I entered into a relationship with a young man. He was also saved, spirit filled and he was active in ministry. We got close really fast and I remember expressing to him my desire to not fornicate and to remain abstinent until marriage and he stated his desire was the same. By this time, it had been nearly two years that I had walked in sexual purity. In my mind we set boundaries because we had this discussion. There was a fear in me that did not want to get close to him because I remembered what it felt like to fall in fornication without intending to. In previous years before I was saved and attended church, I practiced abstinence for various periods throughout my life, religiously. This was something I held a strong conviction about doing but could never last longer than two years at a time.

Although we agreed to remain abstinent, we did not protect ourselves or the relationship from going where we agreed we didn't want it to go. Shortly after we began dating, we started talking on the phone for countless hours, holding hands and kissing. I presented the idea that maybe we should not kiss at all because we both experienced in the past how kissing can lead to fornication. We did not take heed to this suggestion and soon after fell into fornication. Immediately after, I cried and felt convicted of our actions and vowed to never do it again. We remained a couple but committed fornication again a week later. How could we keep falling into the trap of fornication if we vowed not to do it and knew it was wrong? How could we fall into fornication when our intentions were not to have sex until we were married? As believers, how was it possible to fall into sin even though we both felt like we were on fire for God? The answer is simple. We did not set proper boundaries in place to set the standard for our relationship. We had no accountability outside of others knowing we were dating and we were not transparent with the nature of our relationship. We often hung out alone without notifying anyone else we would be hanging out together and crossed multiple boundaries.

No matter how strong, disciplined or saved you are, without setting proper boundaries before you enter into a relationship, sin will be inevitable. The word of God warns us not to trust our flesh (**Galatians 5:19-21, Luke 9:23, Galatians 2:20**). When boundaries are absent, our flesh is present. Setting boundaries in all relationships is necessary to protect it. If it is your desire to walk in purity before marriage, it will not work unless you embrace and implement boundaries in your relationship. Society and the world views boundaries as being controlling and *"too much"*, but the word of God instructs us NOT to trust in our flesh, to FLEE fornication and to live a life that resembles HOLINESS and SANCTIFICATION! Boundaries are created to protect you, the person who you are pursuing and your relationship.

So how are Godly boundaries established in a relationship? You set boundaries by first making sure that you and the person who you are pursuing a relationship with are equally-yoked. A person who does not share your same values of purity before marriage will not be compliant with or embrace your boundaries. Both individuals must have boundaries and it will never work if just one person values boundaries. When entertaining a relationship with someone who does not understand the importance of having boundaries, you will find yourself tempted quite often. You can discuss your boundaries with this person but soon enough they will attempt to talk you into crossing boundaries. People who do not understand or value boundaries, will find it difficulty in helping you to protect yours. Both individuals in the relationship should be on one accord about the boundaries that are being implemented in the relationship. Never leave the issue of boundaries unaddressed or unresolved. If one person has an issue with maintaining boundaries, it may not be wise to move forward with the person.

Boundaries should be clear, without any grey areas. There are several things to consider when setting boundaries. Some general boundaries are:

1. *Do not be led by your emotions*. When a new relationship is evolving, it's exciting. Along with the excitement comes anxiousness to see where the relationship will go. It is important to become aware of your emotions and to not make any decisions based on how you feel. Behaviors and decisions that are emotionally-based usually end in disappointment or regret. The Holy Spirit must be your guide at all times, not your emotions.

2. *Do not become physically involved in your relationship*. There is much debate about whether or not kissing in relationships is biblical or not. My personal opinion is anything that will cause temptation should be eliminated. If we are instructed to *"flee fornication"*, putting ourselves in situations where we are flirting with fornication is unwise. Many will argue kissing is harmless. While kissing is not considered sexual sin, it is a common seed that leads to sexual sin. If your heart is to truly please God and to remain pure before marriage, kissing in any form should be eliminated. When we test or push our limits in boundaries we begin trusting in our flesh. How many times have you heard someone say they did not mean to fornicate but *"it just *happened"?* Being physical or intimate in any way is the sure way to fall into sexual sin. If your potential mate can not go without kissing, rubbing, touching or sleeping with you before entering into a covenant marriage with you, you have bigger problems to consider. There is most likely a spirit of lust resident in him/her and marriage does not heal lust.

3. ***Become aware of how much time you spend with your potential mate***. In new relationships, a desire to see and talk to the person who you are pursuing is inevitable. You want to talk on the phone, go on dates and hang out. Time is very critical in establishing and protecting boundaries. In courtship, you will need to spend time with the other person in order to get to know them and to determine if you are compatible with one another. Most people think the more time, the better. Balance in how much time is spent together should be considered at all times. When entering a new relationship it is very easy to lose focus from priorities and what is important. For example, talking on the phone seems normal in relationships. Talking too much and too long on the phone can present threats to your relationship. It is unwise to talk on the phone until midnight and late into the midnight hours when you have work or school in the morning. Furthermore, talking on the phone with someone who you are attracted to can open doors to lust and fantasy. In order to protect yourself and your relationship, set a reasonable time to have telephone conversations. If you find yourself neglecting your work or school, responsibilities and God, it is an indicator you have crossed some boundaries.

It is also important to consider how much time you spend in person with your potential mate. As unmarried believers it is a boundary issue if you are out together alone in late night hours. Spending a night in the same house, room or bed are also boundary issues. Many will argue they can control themselves, but once again why put your trust in your flesh? There will most certainly be temptations the more you spend time with the person who you are involved with. Some great ways of avoiding temptation is to have others around when possible. If you want to go to an evening show, go with a group of friends and not alone.

4. *Be Transparent*. Transparency is a key factor in determining how successful a relationship will be. If you are entertaining a relationship with a man/woman who refuses to be transparent about their past or present, this is a red flag. A great attribute of a potential mate is their willingness to be transparent with you. No matter how bad their past was, there is safety in being transparent with someone who truly loves you for you. The inability to be transparent with another person is a sign that trust issues are evident. When you love someone, you trust them with your secrets, hopes and dreams. One of the worst feelings in a relationship is to find out something about someone that they tried to hide from you. Transparency and trust is a must!

5. *You need Accountability*. Not only is it imperative to be transparent with the person who you are in a relationship with, but it is important to bring trustworthy people around your relationship for both transparency and accountability purposes. Contrary to popular belief, it is unwise to keep EVERYONE out of your business. Now this does not mean everyone should be in your business; however, someone other than the couple should have some insight into what is going on in your relationship. Not someone who will agree with everything you say and do but a person who is unbiased, has the Holy Spirit and wisdom of God should become your accountability partner. Having accountability will help you to commit to the vows you have made to God concerning the standards you intend to uphold in your relationship. A good accountability partner(s) should be able to challenge you when needed but have your best interest at hand. They should love you enough to tell you the truth! This person is not positioned to control you but to help keep you accountable to your commitments to God and yourself.

So, why are boundaries important? What are the benefits of establishing boundaries? Boundaries can help you to keep your focus and to remain sober in your relationship. In new relationships, it is easy to become distracted by your emotions and to lose sight of what is important to you and God. In order to be lead by the Holy Spirit you must be positioned to hear him consistently. When you are distracted it becomes more difficult to follow and hear God. When you feel like you are in love, your feelings and emotions will be loud and clear. Boundaries will help to amplify God's voice louder and clearer than your flesh and will help you to remain sober in your decision making.

Another benefit of boundaries is that it will teach you self-control. It is God's desire that we all have self-control **(Galatians 5).** A relationship should not cause you to lose yourself or abandon your standards. Sometimes we set high standards when we are not in a relationship but when a potential mate or someone who you are attracted to is present, it's easy to discard those standards. Boundaries will ensure your flesh does not control you but instead it will lead you to conquer your flesh.

There are several other benefits of establishing boundaries in your relationships. It teaches you how to take responsibility for your behaviors, actions and your life. It also serves as protection. Boundaries will protect you from your flesh, the other person's flesh and the traps and temptations the enemy seeks to set up against you. Without Godly boundaries your relationship will start out headed for disappointment. Embracing boundaries will give your relationship the best chance of seeing the other person for who they really are. If your relationship is in fact the will of God, establishing boundaries will help it to flourish and grow!

Chapter 10: In Pursuit of His Will

How can we determine if God supports dating or courtship if neither word is mentioned in the bible? Many Christians believe since the word dating or courtship is not mentioned in the bible, there is no real standard for how believers should entertain relationships. They believe it is up to the individual and it is ok to use whatever technique works best for them. The problem with that belief is that it negates the Word of God. The bible gives reference for EVERY situation that may occur in our lives including relationships and marriage. To accurately answer the question of whether or not God supports dating, courtship or neither, we can take a look to His word.

When we consider the story of Ruth and Boaz, Boaz noticed her and inquired about her **(Ruth 2:5-6).** Immediately after noticing Ruth, Boaz tried to win her heart. He invited her in his fields, offered her water to drink and offered for her to join him for lunch. This act of kindness may not seem like much to us but back then it was a generous gesture. Ruth acknowledged the Christ-like character in Boaz. They both followed the proper protocol that was required back in the day and soon after they got married. A design and procedures were already set in place to protect both people in their pursuit of discovering if they were the will of God for each other. These procedures helped them to keep their relationship pure before marriage. Before they encountered each other for the first time, Ruth became a woman of God and of excellence. She was humble, modest, selfless and she knew how to labor. Boaz on the other hand was a man of God, a protector, provider and was self-disciplined. They were both mature enough for a relationship and submitted it to God.

    The book of *Song of Solomon* is not just a love story between Solomon and a Shulamite girl. It portrays a more detailed example of the Godly design for entertaining a relationship with someone you are pursuing. The first part of the book gives count of how the two carried on their relationship. In chapter 1, we are made aware of both Solomon and the Shulamite girl's attraction to one another. They both acknowledged they wanted to be together and only had eyes for one another. During their courtship period, the couple expressed their love for one another, respected and admired each other, learned about one another and strengthened their bond for one another. Their courtship did not just involve the two but they also included others. They included their friends and family. In chapter 1 verse 7, you see the Shulamite girl consulting with her shepherd.

In this love story, we also see how the two are tempted but are careful of not falling into fornication. **Verses 2:7, 3:5**, and **8:4** all express the same idea. All three verses place an emphasis on this statement, *"do not stir up or awaken love until it please"*. To stir in this context means to *excite strong feelings*. This scripture speaks volumes. It addresses the issue of God's timing as well as remaining pure until you are married. The couple established boundaries in order to remain pure before they got married. The boundaries included not putting themselves in situations that would feed their temptations and by including others to help govern their relationship. Both individuals in the relationship knew what they wanted when they started out. They chose to love one another and their pursuit was marriage. They included Godly principles in how they entertained one another. They were committed to each other from the beginning and honored one another. They were not confused in what they wanted and only had feelings and eyes for each other. Their pursuit of marriage was clear from the beginning and they received confirmation from God and those who they were accountable to.

The love story portrayed in Song of Solomon is one that portrays the principles of courtship. Although the process of marrying back then was a little different from today, the principles remain the same, if unmarried believers are to entertain relationships by Godly standards. It's easy to do relationships the way of the world, but it takes those who desire the heart of God for their lives to adopt Godly standards and principles. There are too many believers who live without any standards as it pertains to relationships and who they choose to marry. When you are in pursuit of His will for your life, it is important that you adopt and embrace His standards and His principles.

Despite controversies of what is acceptable in dating, courtship and marriage, the Word of God gives believers a framework of how we are to live, what kind of relationships we are to have and the type of person we are to walk in covenant with. There are numerous scriptures in the bible that portray characteristics of a Godly husband and a Godly wife. This should be our standard. The Word of God also shows us how all of our relationships should be influenced by and aim to glorify God. The Word of God instructs us of who we are to entertain relationships with and those who we are not. No matter what the world says, God's Word will always remain the standard for how we are to live our lives and conduct relationships. If we desire relationships that are in His will, we must pursue relationships HIS way!

Prior to men pursuing women or women positioning themselves to be found by a potential mate, it is imperative that both individuals pursue God wholeheartedly. Without the pursuit of Christ prior to entertaining relationships with the intention of marriage, it is impossible to pursue the will of God for your life including what person is the will of God for you. Every individual must first understand who true love is before pursuing an earthly love. Jesus Christ should be your first *"True Love"* and through gaining a consistent and stable relationship with Him, men are able to pursue the woman who is the will of God for his life and women are able to identify if the man who pursues her is the will of God for her life. The truth is true love can only be found in and through Christ Jesus.

No matter if you are unmarried, engaged or married, if you have submitted your life to Christ and have allowed him to become the number one priority in your life, you have already discovered true love. For every unmarried man and woman who feels inadequate, forgotten, unloved and unwanted because you are not in a relationship or married, remember God loves you more than anyone in this world possibly could and longs to be the first love of your life. There is no other love greater than the love of God, and as you continue waiting on the Lord and remaining in His will, remember he has your best interest at hand. Discovering the one who is love is the best kind of love you could ever experience in your life. God is TRUE LOVE! When you discover and encounter true love, you lose the desire to do anything or connect with anyone outside of His will for your life. True love has taught me that Jesus and His will for my life is more than enough for me!

"In Pursuit of His Will: The Journey of Finding True Love"

"Prayers for the Unmarried"

Father God,

I thank you that our identity is in Christ Jesus and we are not defined by our marital status or materialistic things, but we are defined by you. Lord, I thank your for the blessings you continually bestow upon our lives and we are grateful for your unconditional love for us. Father, you are already aware of those who are unmarried and their heart's desire so I ask that you would enable every unmarried man and woman to submit their desires to you in exchange for what you desire for their lives. Remove every ungodly desire and idol in their hearts for relationships and marriage. You are a God of covenant and the creator of relationships and marriage, therefore I pray that those who desire marriage your way, will give every potential relationship to you for your counsel and guidance. Remove all blinders from their eyes that would prohibit them from seeing counterfeits for who they really are and help them to not be anxious for any relationship other than their relationship with you. Help them to guard their hearts and keep them healthy (spiritually and naturally) from being contaminated and defiled by the perspectives and ways of the world. Help them to walk in purity until you join them to their future wives and husbands. Lord, we trust you know what is best for every unmarried person.

Help them to submit their future completely into your hands. For those who will become husbands/wives in the future, prepare and equip them to become the best husband/wife they could possibly be. Help every unmarried man and women who desires marriage your way, to remain in their place of obscurity until you are ready to send their mates. Help them to focus on you and your plans for their lives. Help them to not see being unmarried as a curse but as a blessing during this season of their lives. Help them to take joy in the many blessings you have provided them with and to pursue your kingdom with all they have. Help every unmarried man and woman to make good use of the time you have blessed them with before you send their future mates. Father, I thank you that you will lead and guide them and as they submit their lives completely to you. Order their steps and cause your will and plans to manifest in their lives, in your timing. Amen.

~ Marquitta Rodgers

Co-Founder of The Unmarried Movement

"Prayers for the Unmarried"

Father God,

We thank you for your word, for heaven and earth shall past but your word shall remain. Now let the power of your word bring forth the light of truth and revelation to the unmarried. Let there be an outpouring of your might that falls upon the unmarried, and cause them to stand in the strength of the Lord and in a place of purity.

May the oil of resistance come so that we will resist the tricks, plots and plans of the enemy, that we will refuse to give in, refuse to accept or comply with distractions and assignments from hell. We thank you for the strength to withstand damaging acts and decision that can separate us from your Glory. We thank you that we have the strength to say no to temptations before it arise.

On behalf of the unmarried, I thank you for this season of growth and prosperity, I thank you for a place of soberness, a place where we are aware that we can't do anything apart from you, I pray that we present our bodies as a living sacrifice, holy, acceptable unto you which is our reasonable service, and that we will not be conformed to this world: but be transformed by the renewing of our mind, that we may prove what is good, acceptable, and the perfect will of God according to **Romans 12:1-2**.

I thank you that we are strengthened in you and make a bold declaration that there is no temptation taken us but such as is common to man: we know that you God are faithful, you will not suffer us to be tempted above what we are able, but with every temptation that God has given us a way to escape and the ability to withstand accordingly to **1 Corinthian 10:13**.

I decree that righteous living is our portion, a life of holiness free from adultery, fornication, masturbation, pornography, and all unauthorized activity that will cause us to fall from this place of righteous living in you. Let us live a life of holiness, a life style that is pleasing unto God. We will live a life of righteousness, purification, compromising will not be known amongst us.

Lord, I speak wisdom over us that will cause us to function in a place filled with peace (nothing broken, nothing missing) and when the enemy of loneliness comes in like a flood and tries to cause us to lose focus on the call and purpose of the kingdom, the Spirit of the LORD shall lift up a standard against him according to Isaiah 59:19.

I decree that by the name of Jesus Christ that we all speak the same thing, and there is no division amongst us, we will be joined together perfectly in the same mind and in the same judgment (1Cor1:10), may the unmarried operate in strong discernment, we will discern the wolf in sheep clothing, we will not listen to the voice of our flesh, we will obey the voice of God concerning, today, tomorrow, our future and the promises of God for us, we will flee temptation and cast down every vain imagination that will exalt itself against the will of God every memory recall spirit that will have us to daydream and reminisce about past experience and relationship that will draw us in the fantasy realm. We are committed to being a sold out people and we will be anxious for nothing, we will await until the appointed time.

We will grid the loins of our mind, be sober and hope. We will dedicate our lives, energy and time to the advancement of the Kingdom of God and to adhere to the Godly counsel of the righteous, our leaders, Elders and others. We will take all necessary steps and make the proper adjustments in our lives that will prepare us for Ministry, counsel and marriage, the unmarried men will be known for their Valor, and the unmarried woman will be known in the courtyard as virtuous. As obedient children we will not fashion ourselves according to former lusts in our ignorance, for you are holy and we are Holy in all manner of communication.

~ **Verna Steele**

Co-Founder of The Unmarried Movement

"Prayers for the Unmarried"

To the Unmarried,

You are amazing. You are precious to the eyes of Jesus. I pray for every unmarried individual that they will be purposed to love and pursue the heart of God for their life and legacy. I cover the mind and heart of every unmarried person that they will not be distracted by the pattern of the world, but to understand that they are to live according to the blueprint in the word of God to live holy.I declare that they will be strong in abstaining from sexual immorality and understand that their purity is not something to be ashamed of but to wear as a badge of honor because they are to be set apart and sanctified. I declare that their mind and body will be submitted to the Lord.

I thank you for the unmarried individuals that will fall in love with Jesus first, prior to searching for the heart of a spouse. I pray that right relationships and covenant friendships will be formed to encourage, build, and push them in to the destiny of God. I declare that they will stand for who they are in Christ Jesus and not to be ashamed of their marital status but to use this season of life to explore, live and discover the depths and heights of God for their life.
I thank you God that when the time comes to meet their spouse that they will have proper accountability and will be submitted to the Holy

Spirit so that they can build the next generation of lovers of Jesus Christ. Thank you for this world changer and that they will be uninhibited to be an impact in the world for Christ.
1 Peter 2:9; **Romans 12:2**; **Philippians 4:8**

~Ivey N. Smith
Co-Founder of The Unmarried Movement
Owner of "MY Identity" Clothing and Accessories

"In Pursuit of His Will: The Journey of Finding True Love"

Father, I thank you for the men today who have set themselves to become the man you have destined them to be. I declare **Psalm 139** over each of them, that they will know who there God is. They will embrace You as their Creator, and will love others how you love them. May they be confident in their manhood not allowing anything to comprise their integrity, purity, or their relationship with You! I declare they will be free from the hindrances and memories of the past, and press on toward the upward call of Christ Jesus!

~ Jamal Miller
Co-founder of MarriedandYoung.com
www.jamalmiller.com
www.marriedandyoung.com

"In Pursuit of His Will: The Journey of Finding True Love"

Dear Heavenly Father,

I thank you for every unmarried woman who desires to be married. I pray that you give them the strength & courage to wait on your perfect timing. I ask that during their season of waiting they will remain encouraged and confident in You. I pray that they would enjoy you and your presence and that their relationship with you would continue to grow and mature in their relationship with you. Thank you for what you are doing in their lives Lord. Amen.

~ Natasha Miller
Co-founder of MarriedandYoung.com

"In Pursuit of His Will: The Journey of Finding True Love"

Lord,
 I thank you that according to **Jeremiah 29:11** you know the plans for us, and because we choose to stay pure before you, you are with us and will strengthen us in our times of weakness. I thank you Lord that because we have chosen to be equally yoked and keep our eyes upon you, you will grant us the desires of our heart. Lord, we know your word says it is not good for a man to be alone and that you make a helper fit for all who desire. We choose to go through the process in which you have chosen for us and we will not be anxious for anything but in everything we will stand in your court as priests until you show us the one who you have chosen for us. Even when the enemy comes in to sway and distract us, we will stand upon your word and stay pure until the appointed time in which we leave our father and mother to hold fast to our wife and become one in the flesh and spirit. Amen

~ Robert Champion

"In Pursuit of His Will: The Journey of Finding True Love"

Father in the name of Jesus, I declare and decree that every unmarried woman that read this book that the eyes of your understanding be flooded with light and that you fully understand you are a capable, intelligent, and virtuous woman and you are far more precious than jewels and your value is far above rubies or pearls. I declare you are a woman who has a relationship with Jesus Christ and you know Him as Abba Father and you understand who you are in Him. I declare and decree you are a woman of the word, a woman of prayer, a woman of fasting, a woman in pursuit of purpose, a woman that has wisdom beyond your years, a woman of integrity and a woman of character. I declare you are sensitive to hearing and leading of The Holy Spirit and you will never do anything outside the will of The Lord. I declare and decree your discernment is sharp in the spirit therefore, you will never be tricked nor deceived by the devil when he tries to send a counterfeit disguised as your husband and that you are able to identify the true from the false; the real from the fake; the clean from the unclean and a holy one from one who is profaned. I declare and decree like Ruth, you will follow instruction and be found working in the Kingdom of God. I declare and decree your focus will be on the things of God and His purpose for your life. I declare and decree you are surrounded by a multitude of counselors that you remain safe at all times. I declare and decree that you are a woman who

"In Pursuit of His Will: The Journey of Finding True Love"

is found and not one who chases after a man. I declare when you become a wife that the heart of her husband trusts in you confidently and relies on and believes in you securely, so that he has no lack of honest gain or need of dishonest spoil. I declare and decree you are a woman who comforts, encourages, and does your husband only good as long as there is life within you as his wife. I declare you are a woman who has vision, one who rises early and prepare your day by rises while it is still night and prepare spiritual food for your family and command your day. I declare you are one who understands when to invest and when not to invest; that you may remain fruitful. I declare you are a woman girded with strength (spiritual, mental, and physical fitness for your God-given task) and may your arms be strong and firm for your spiritual assignment in the earth. I declare your husband is known in the city's gates, that he is one of Godly influence and affluence, one of integrity and character and most of all a mighty man of valor in The Lord. I declare and decree your husband will have favor throughout the land and in due time he will find you as his good thing. I declare the both of you are clothed in strength and in dignity and the both of you are secure in the Lord. I declare and decree in your mouth is skillful and godly wisdom and on your tongue is the law of kindness – one who can give counsel and instruction. I declare and decree that you are not an idle woman, one sits around and gossip, but a woman who strategically prepares for the future of your household. I declare and decree your children will rise up early and call you blessed. May the fruit of your hands continue to be blessed as you take this journey with The Lord as an unmarried woman and throughout your days as a married woman.

Kingdom Blessings,

Prophetess Kisha L. Cephus

Contact Me

Feel free to send me a message through any of the following link:

> mrodge20@yahoo.com

> mrodge20@gmail.com

> https://m.facebook.com/The-unmarriedmovement

Made in the USA
San Bernardino, CA
05 December 2014